shankara

spandaloka

SL

CONTENTS

Foreword By John Mann	07
Introduction	09
PROLOGUE: Divine Life	17
PART I: EVERYBODY'S HEAVEN	20
A Short Spiritual Autobiography	
1. The Taste Of Incompleteness	22
2. The Limits Of Experience	26
3. Reality's Merciless Love	30
4. The Discipline Of Rapture	33
5. Satisfaction Infinite	36
6. Spandaloka Gateway	38
PART II: THE IMPULSE OF LOVE UNTOLD	42
7. The „Rise" Of The Most Real	45
8. The Two Kinds Of Restlessness And The Twofold Meaning Of Life	47
9. The „Happiness" Trap And Its Ecstatic Antidote	52
10. The Existential Dive	58
11. Wanting The Most Real	61
12. The In-Love-State	64

PART III: SPANDALOKA 66

13. The Most Intimate 69
14. The Most Real 75
15. The Most Obvious 80

PART IV: RADIANT BEING 88

16. The Secret Of Divine Realization 91
17. Radiant Existence 95
18. The Chidakash Sutras 100

EPILOGUE: Truth And Grace 109

In The Mouth Of Her Light 116

The Light Of The World 118
The Spanda Grand 121
Spanda Invocation 124

The Stages Of The Realization Process 127
Further Information 130

Foreword By John Mann

There are many ways for the reader to approach this book: as a Scholar, a Philosopher, a Linguist, a Theologian, a Spiritual Practitioner or simply as a human being.

There are also many ways of describing the book itself:

As a Non-Dualistic Vedantically-oriented text to be viewed within that ancient Hindu tradition.

As a carefully worded description of the inherent dilemma of the human condition.

As an original prescription for the resolution of that condition.

Perhaps the best way to view <u>Spandaloka</u> is as a Scripture; a prophetic document that appears out of the mist and that tends to leave the reader with the over-riding question:

„<u>IS IT REALLY TRUE?</u>"

It left me with that question, but I have gradually realized that „Truth" is not the essential issue, because even if every word is correct, it doesn't necessarily change anything. It simply casts our human situation into a clearer focus.

So what is the most essential question in reference to what you are about to read?

I would suggest that it is:

"How does it affect you in the depth of your Being?"

There is no way to know that in advance and it may not affect you very much unless you are open to receive whatever message it transmits.

But if you are willing to let go of whatever preconceptions you possess, then you will be free to enjoy a voyage of discovery: intellectual, emotional, perceptual and most important, spiritual: Achieving a sense of reality that you may have suspected to be true, but which, with the exception of an occasional glimpse, has always been hidden off-stage, patiently waiting to appear.

May Spandaloka open the door.

John Mann – 2/24/2016

Dr. John Mann was a lifelong student of Rudi, or Swami Rudrananda (Albert Rudolph), a well-known art dealer and spiritual teacher.

A social psychologist by training, Dr. Mann taught for many years at New York University and SUNY Geneseo, and is the author of more than fifteen books, including *Before the Sun: Meeting Rudi*, *Sigmund Freud: Doctor of Secrets and Dreams*, and *Frontiers of Psychology*.

Introduction

This book does *not* contain a religious teaching. It does not contain a teaching *at all*. Rather, it is a Reality Revelation. Thus, it can and should be treated as truth or Truth, that can and should prove itself with undeniable experiential Facticity and Onticity.

If science is the endeavor that designates the discovery of *knowledge* through facts, experiments, observation and experience, and if knowledge is living *reality* information, then science is the way or value measuring process to apply in order to validate, what this book is about and what it says, and neither a kind of belief or faith in the sense of blind trust nor a just personally determined preference or taste.

On the one hand a fact is not always an *absolute*, because the experience of somebody who hallucinates is factual as long as the hallucination lasts.

Furthermore, even if somebody is not in an obvious hallucination, the fact that there is a vision or experience of a spiritual or metaphysical or psychological or transpersonal entity, figure or reality or state, which belongs to a specific religion or teaching, doesn't mean that this experiential fact is an absolute *fact*, because in such a case the unconscious is mixing whatever is really happening with a specific religious or teaching *conditioning*.

On the other hand, if philosophical games of the kind of denying any fact whatsoever (because we could for example merely be brains in a vat convinced of what is experienced as *the reality*) interfere with the validity of any science or any similar endeavor whatsoever, there is no other choice than rejecting such games.

It *is* possible to reject such games and it *is* possible to rely on facticity and onticity, which truly and undeniably exist. *Clarity* is the key. What kind of clarity? How can you be and stay clear?

Be and stay as clear as the fact that what you are reading right now *is being read* by you.

Be and stay as clear as the fact that when you *are* thirsty, you <u>are</u> *thirsty*.

Be and stay as clear as the fact that humans *have* two legs and so on.

Be and stay as clear as the reason that relies on the laws of reality disclosed and described by physics, chemistry and what is before, inside and beyond them.

Based on *this* kind of the factually real, biology, zoology, anthropology, psychology, sociology and all the relevant sciences of a true culture, are the disciplines to be involved in the validation and disclosure of the Spiritual Reality and Process I am talking about.

The term ‚spiritual' in my case is meant in the Sense of *Spirit as Kundalini Mahashakti*, Which Is The Vibrant Force, Field Or Space As Main and First Agent Of <u>Radiant Paramrita Spanda</u>, Which Is The First And Transcendentally Free And Everything Else Generating and Containing Reality.

What I am actually *talking* about here?

Exactly this is, what needs to be disclosed and experienced and ontically realized and validated by those who strongly and sufficiently *feel* its attractivity and its reality.

Exactly this is what this book is about: Transcendental Spiritual Realization, Existence, Life and Culture Individually and Collectively.

Because I regard it as the most true necessity to be understood and realized. And this because it is the Most Attractive Manner of Existing and the only true Reality Culture.

After my (rather short) autobiography, which mainly contains the spiritually relevant and quite generally valid events and aspects of my life until now (Part I), I describe principles and truths, that are important to understand, feel, embody, realize and be in order for the Spiritual Realization and Liberation Process to unfold towards its natural blossoming (Part II).

In the next Part of the book (III) I describe the anatomy of Transcendental Spiritual Reality and Corresponding Or Coincident Truths towards Its Realization in a direct and systematic manner, as this anatomy „Wanted" to be Expressed In And Through „My" or In And Through The Spanda or Radiant Reality State.

This continues in the last main Part (IV), in which I include further writings, that spontaneously „wanted" to contribute to this book of special aim.

Welcome to Spandaloka. Welcome to The Realm Of Spanda. Welcome to The Real World In Its True Freedom And In Its True Light.

Don't just believe me. Validate and verify everything I say. Guided by the strongest and fullest clarity possible, upon which you can feel, discover, practice and experience, how to *Open* to *Get* Realized *By Her*.

Nityananda Of Ganeshpuri

„Whoever studies carefully,
finds Liberation in this life.
Whoever studies like a wild elephant,
finds only delusion."

―――――――――――

Sri Bhagavan Nityananda
Of Ganeshpuri

Prologue: Divine Life

1.

The Divine Life Is so Full, Tender, Blissful and Sweet, that It Transcends every single one of your past dreams and every single one of your future dreams.

2.

The Divine Life Is so True, Real, Infinite and Free, that every attempt or even intention to describe It or to imagine It or to even feel It, will necessarily „modify" It, „alter" It, „distort" It and thus „reduce" It and thereby „make" It or rather „degenerate" It to a *thing*.

3.

The Divine Life Is *The* Way-To-Be, that, once „discovered" or truly *re*-cognized, will never be denied again, because it *can never* be denied again!

4.

When you are once Touched by The Divine Life, you will *never* again want *anything more* than It. It „Will" most naturally „Undermine" the ultimate effect of every other possible want or need.

5.

As a matter of fact It „Will" dissolve every other *need* for ultimate satisfaction, love and fulfillment, because It *Transcends* every other need for ultimate satisfaction, love and fulfillment.

6.

This doesn't mean that It merely Exists or Goes *Beyond* every other need for ultimate satisfaction, love and fulfillment, but that It Is also *Prior* to every other need for ultimate satisfaction, love and fulfillment.

7.

This Is The Case, because It Goes Beyond and Is Prior to *Everything* and because It *Is* Ultimate Satisfaction, Love and Fulfillment *Itself*.

8.

Every conceivable of your possibilities or attempts to reach and attain ultimate satisfaction, love and fulfillment and be nurtured with ecstasy *outside* The Divine Domain, is therefore your hidden and covered cry *for The Divine*.

9.

Every conceivable of your possibilities or attempts to reach and attain ultimate satisfaction, love and fulfillment and be nurtured with ecstasy *outside* The Divine Domain, is the sign of your desperate and *strongest* and Essentially Ecstatic Need for The *Most Real* and *Most Blissful* Nourishment and Shine.

Part I

Everybody's Heaven

A Short Spiritual Autobiography

I am coming from The Most Intimate Unknown. Unrooted Deep Fountain Bliss, Transcending every dimension or notion of space, time and cause.

My appearing personal history may very well imply features, hints and signs of catalytic value for anyone unavoidably attracted to The Divine Self-Recognition Process.

My Spiritual Function though operates on the basis of the Irrefutable Laws of Divine Realization, which were at work before „My" „Big Bang" and have been fully understood by „me" in retrospect.

These Laws are always there. They can be discovered by everybody. They are undeniably and self-evidently Illuminating Truths. About being human as such, about Reality Itself and about all that is necessary to be understood and realized, so that The Divine Can Transcendentally Recognize Itself As A Human Expression.

Therefore, this short spiritual autobiography elucidates the special stream of events or aspects that appear to be relevant insofar as they shaped *my* spiritual process and at the same time as they seem to be *general* components of the Realization Process *Itself*.

1. The Taste Of Incompleteness

As a child I was wondering. I was fully alive. Uncorrupted vital presence. I was energy thriving on its own.

Yet at the same time, looking around and observing the world and the doings of humans, I was puzzled: *„Is that all? Is this how life is supposed to be? Is this how life* *really is? What are all these people doing? How can they seriously be satisfied through re-enacting this same dull exercise?"* That was the mood that defined my conscious reality.

Mentally I might have concluded for moments this *could* be all. This „reasonable" conclusion however made no impression whatsoever to the living energy I was. On the contrary. It dynamized my impulse to find out, what's going on. It forced it up.

*

Embedded in the culture I was born into and deluded by uninspected cultural and humanly-motivationally confused forces, I had no genuine feedback from reality other than through the energy that was constituting me and everything around me, as this was accessible via the body-mind-apparatus I was identified with or rather reduced to: my conscious and unconscious senses, my emotional body and my intuition.

The very deep Transcendental Yearning, waiting eternally behind the veil of the cyclic cultural routine, whenever it would tenderly shine through, was only consoled and never really satisfied. This consolation was taking place in different ways:

In the emotional connection to other human beings or living organisms or the entirety of living reality.

In my linguistic exploration of the psychic realm in the form of writing poetry or essays.

In the deep affection for the magical transformations of felt reality through music.

In my thirst for knowledge, to be found in books or

encyclopedias.

In the vital expression of the energy I was: while playing, or dancing, or running, or exploring the nature around our town.

In all that culture, science, religion, mythology and art were offering as an experiential configuration to get immersed in or hypnotized by.

*

No doubt that consolation and hypnosis, as – from the point of view of Radical Truth – main delusional gravitational forces, achieved their contribution in permanently suppressing my all-encompassing Core Need.

But suppressing something, which cannot be forgotten, and this for a long time, in my case only accumulated the aggravation of my patience or my willingness to endure the confusion and meaninglessness of existence.

At the same time, during all those childhood and teenage years, the smell of the ecstasy of reality never ceased to tempt my root identity. In the midst of all the pain inside me and in the faces of my fellow humans something never left. And I could sense the same in almost everybody else.

*

It was no wonder then for my consistent uneasiness – especially since there was nobody to turn to, who could solve the problem – to start to try piercing through the stifling atmosphere of transcendental emptiness.

The first window, through which I could reach out to the open and escape from the local religiosity and the knowledge in the available books and of the people around me, was a magazine on parapsychology. Its content was never meant to become a real interest of mine, but it contained a little bit with an aura that was able to feed my unconscious impulse to continue the search.

Whenever a promise for a deeper look into reality would show up, I would snap at the chance. It is for example easy to remember my father's schock, when the postman came and asked for some hundred dollars for the delivery of a package filled with books. Which I had ordered... Yes, I had the money, which was all I earned working in a nearby factory in a summer of my middle high school years. At least the money was just enough for the twenty, and all esoteric, books. And all this because their author seemed to know about a deeper and truer reality. The books really didn't change anything, but this whole anecdote is symptomatic for what I was ready to invest for Truth.

*

An intense thirst for Truth was governing my inner search, a thirst for pure and substantial reality that *had* to be there.

It was easier to intuit such reality, when I was drifting in the paradisiac scent of the adventurous landscape around my town. But it was vanishing behind or below the emotional reactivity and neediness that was predominantly pulling the strings whenever I was in the midst of gatherings of relatives and friends.

Many times, when I was alone, sometimes even in gatherings I would retreat to an unobserved spot, I would sit with either closed or opened eyes and I would let my whole body-mind feel ever closer to the most direct feeling possible, as if I was about to find the first feeling possible of *being* there, the first feeling possible of *being*.

2. The Limits Of Experience

The teenage life completed, and starting a new adventure in the university and at the same time being on my own, away from home and free, life didn't change radically, even though it became more colorful and varied in its cultural and social aspect.

The most significant change was to get to know new different personalities, new combinations of cultural, anthropological and psychological aspects. And this was fascinating. And it never stopped to be fascinating: how every single person was and is a unique reality, a whole different world.

At the same time all these different worlds were sharing one reality. So there I was, in the same „game", but with some new levels, additional variations and some upgraded rules. The name of the „game": existing. The context of the „game": reality.

My new targeted source of new and hopefully decisive knowledge for life and transcendental clarity were professors of linguistics, semantics, philosophy, religion, logic and consciousness research. These were also the areas I was automatically drawn to in the huge multi-leveled university library, in which I was spending most of my afternoons in my first university years.

The body-mind problem, the neurological substratum of perception, the symbolic interconnectedness of innumerable meaningful elements of being in the world, the exhausting variety of the dependence of understanding on an always different perspective, and yet, the common, if not same, existential characteristics or attributes of human reality.

*

Parallel to all these crucial discoveries and deeper insights, the driving force, which would later immensely or primarily contribute to the transcendental spiritual events to take place, was in part an unconscious „gravitational" dimension that could be named *the natural state...*

‚Nature' or ‚natural', if understood as attributes of the real, in the sense of *how things are supposed to be according to their nature*, was the compass of the continuation of my search. I started, especially while and after reading and getting immersed into various metaphysical or ontological texts of occidental philosophy and oriental or especially hinduistic spirituality, to relax bodily or, let me say, energetically.

But whatever the relaxation or restful satisfaction, my tranquil state always would eventually get disturbed again; in an inevitable cycle; in a sisyphean inescapability. A new phase was about to start in my life.

Apart from an ever deepening understanding and

an ever liberated intuition of the logic of reality, what was mostly occupying my attention or the concentration of consciousness connected to my body-mind in the years before and after the university, was the plasticity of this consciousness or of the existential field that was constituted by whatever constituents outside my control and was constituting the however modified character of the respective experiential content.

In other words it was both fascinating and disheartening to always amazed, but helplessly realize, how the interactive chemistry of the world and the psyche would radically reshape the mood of this very psyche and of this very world. Emotion was the ruler; or the weaver of the fabric of existence.

*

The vicissitude of reality or its mood, based both on the ongoing organismic change of the body-mind and the emotional pervasiveness, which is being configured by any different given situation, for a long time generated the reasonable conclusion, that if it is the case, that reality or even the whole world feels always different, whenever a new emotional chemistry would create a whole different world mood, then what was necessary to find inside this relative chaos or persistent instability was a *constant*; something that would *not* change, even if existentially and experientially everything was changing all the time.

What a paradox... And yet, it was a logical conclusion. It made sense. It was undoubtedly a natural need, to want to cling to something immutably stable. But, as it would be revealed to me years later, this was not the point at all. Liberation had and has nothing to do with escaping or distancing oneself from change. On the contrary: *full participation in* and undifferentiated *identification with natural* change is one of the main prerequisites for the process towards Transcendental Spiritual Liberation...

*

Enveloped by the challenges and developing fascinations of adulthood, in the longer phase that preceded the decisive liberating year, I largely was growing and advancing in the actualization of my human potential. I observed main principles and drives of human behavior, mostly retrospectively.

The deep biology and transcendental meaningfulness of intimacy, communion and connectedness between human beings, living beings and beings of any kind was prevalent. Both in my personal and professional relationships. Innumerable lessons invaded the totality of my mind and psyche.

I always looked in the past for all possible kinds of human experience. Many of them I repeated again and again, sometimes voluntarily, sometimes compulsively. In both cases though it dawned on me, that whether in freedom or in the compulsive prison, I really was not deciding anything myself. This led to yet another radical insight.

I remember sitting in the balcony, on a balmy spring afternoon, when I felt how the usual split inside the totality of energy that the body-mind and everything around it was a part of, was totally or at least quite strongly removed. Such that everything became time itself. The stream of „Schopenhauer's" will. The movement of manifested reality itself as a free „flow" of vibrancy.

*

I cannot recollect all the kinds of satoris or transcendental awakenings, that mostly were happening without me expecting them at all, in the last years of my spiritual search. What I can recollect though was the ceaseless intensification of the search. Its force grew unbearably. And with it the frustration and the suffering grew.

Philosophy, culture and science had been thoroughly examined. For years and years.

Spiritual literature had been exhaustively researched and contemplated upon.

Meditative endeavors and corresponding body work as well.

The encounters with different degrees of human or living or otherwise modified agents of Transcendental Reality were strong and numerous too.

The psychophysical possibilities and dimensions of human experience had also been abundantly explored.

No wonder then, that what happened, happened.

3. Reality's Merciless Love

Thirty-five years behind me, I was working with a group of people in the late afternoon. It was early March, a cloudy sky, we all were engaged in a routine activity.

It was a certain moment, while everything was going as usual and my perception wandered out of the window for some seconds, when the world fell on me. And inside me. And took me down to the hell of futility. The cosmos had shaken. And I was smashed.

As a matter of fact, spiritually, transcendentally, concerning Transcendental Spiritual Realization and Liberation, I had failed. I was hopelessly done. I was finished.

It was an entirely energetic event; and this holistically. It came out of the blue. And no doubt that there were various components previously leading to it, but at that moment, all of them were perfectly buried inside the deepest forest of „my" unconscious reality.

If I am to put in words what happened, Reality spoke to me: „My dear boy, forget it. You cannot control me; to get what you want. Ever". And She, Reality, was saying this in absolute clarity and infinite love at the same time. Well, „good", but the problem was, She didn't give any hint whatsoever for what should be done...

An insufferable frustration had dominated literally everything, permeating all of the reality mood there was. For the following days and weeks after that afternoon I felt dead, a walking incarnation of sorrow, and I had no other choice than coming to terms with the bitter facticity: this is it. There's no liberation. So get realistic, accept the facts, and live this life as it is. There is no transcendental liberation. Forget it. Move on.

The force and power of this emotional death was such that there was no impulse – inside the field of all the energy that was constituting me – towards an attempt to try anything. The realization of the futility of everything

I tried was so powerful, that any reaction from my side, even unconsciously, it seemed, was impossible. In fact I didn't realize anything of all that myself or on my own, it was gigantically pressed into me, beyond any imaginable possibility to react or counteract.

The natural consequence was that everything I thought I knew or had realized was gone. It was washed away by this cataclysmic reality crash through me and through my whole world. An emptiness, a darkness, a void had spread everywhere.

This terribly burning existential devastation, capitulation, resignation and surrender though turned out to become the Spiritually most purifying crisis in my life up to then. It was *the* turning point *per se*. The Radical Conversion Event. Which, at that time, was not clear to me at all.

*

The unprecedented void that emerged out of this Radical Conversion was existential and spiritual emptiness and death. On the other hand, this emptiness was at the same time the catalyst for a massive detoxication, which turned to dust all of the formerly accumulated assumed „knowledge".

This took some weeks. Nobody would notice anything. I continued living my daily life and taking responsibility of the work and what was necessary daily. And then something new started.

I already somehow had got used to the „new" emptiness of life. But I didn't immediately recognize the relief that came with that. It was April now, the scent of spring in the air, my diet was changing, my body wanting to run and do some bodily yoga, and I was enjoying the non-transcendental, the „mundane" joys life had to offer and which every day is full of. And although spiritual stuff was passé, it happened again, yet with no expectation or desire this time, that a spiritual line here or there in a book would catch my attention; like the daily newspaper would do too. In an innocent, pure, desireless way.

In general I was like a young boy with his mouth wide open, when looking at this or that, as if life was new, as if I had never been there before. Everything was interesting. Everything was a little wonder. And exactly that was, what had started, and what I was to understand fully only in the future: The year of wonders started.

4. The Discipline Of Rapture

Quite every single event or even object was, in its simplicity and purity, a revelation.

It could be the unmediated, direct feeling connection with a person; even when a person was not present.

It could be a smile, a bird, an animal in the park, the wind, music, most ordinary activities, just everything.

And it could be „just" me, being me. First bodily, physically and then emotionally, with all that was there, which was energetically „liquid", free to be as it was, to feel itself as it was, so fully, that it would do that without me doing it. It was happening by itself; it was strange, or at least yet unknown, since my attention would only sometimes get caught in observing what was happening, most of the time it was so free and unbound, that the usual dichotomy or division or separation (inside the perceptual activity) between my perceiving me and anything perceived was vanished, was „mysteriously" removed.

This removed separation of the usual perceptual dichotomy opened and initiated just about everything that was to become a whole year of most attractive spiritual practice, although I was not conscious or knowledgeable about it being a practice during that whole year, since it was so attractive and fulfilling, and practice I knew before as something that was requiring discipline and effort and struggle and all the like; but that process was happening on its own...

Thus, it only *later* made sense. It only later showed itself to be the only real practice. Real spiritual practice is most attractive, mainly because it always is real. It always smells like, feels like truth and is true practice or The Work Of Truth; whether it is attached to a happy or not so pleasant experience in a given moment or situation.

*

Words and normal communication cannot match what was happening. But that doesn't matter at all. I will write it as it now wants to express itself.

What I called this process that would go on for about a year, the year of wonders, when I was spontaneously writing about it some years later for my own mind, was *radical authenticity*.

To get to the heart of it, the dilemma that was creating my suffering or deepest uneasiness, was being dissolved at its root regularly, again at again.

By the way, let me briefly mention who I found to be doing all this. Because it wasn't me or „me" at all.

Always I had the feeling that something „out" „there" was guiding me unmistakenly. After the Radical Conversion Event I was in awe to get confirmed and reassured in an initially tender suspicion, but then unparalleled and direct discovery: what was guiding me or „me", was Reality Herself.

She would show Herself in the past in a mediated manner through whatever means and often through human agents, especially, in my case, through the manifestation, which was referred to with the name Bhagavan Nityananda (of Ganeshpuri).

She did everything from the very beginning. And it seems that the configuration of events and circumstances in my life were such, that I was led to the point of giving up constructing a reality; I was forced to give up, and when I did, immediately after that I was seamlessly taken over by Her. And this ‚I' was first the functional and eventually the cosmic ‚I'.

So, what really happened in my case, was that the responsible events and circumstances necessary to initiate this Liberation Process *By Her*, were there, sequentially, and ultimately coming together to a degree of sufficient maturity. In „reality" She, Reality Herself, „Did" All and Everything, And Was and Is All and Everything and Infinitely and Unspeakably and Inconceivably More Than That. To explain this further is a subject in itself, and bigger than the spot in this story here makes possible.

5. Satisfaction Infinite

With the verbal description „radical authenticity" I am referring to the dissolution both of (1) the inner or functional dichotomy inside the usual perceptual activity and through the sticky direction of attention to something, that creates the illusion of identification with the receiver of perception, and (2) of the boundaries between the apparent psychophysical me and the entire world and the totality of existence this ‚me' is embedded in and is an expression of.

The Truth and Validity of this process would be supported from and simultaneously confirmed by quite some passages in the Gitas, in Shaivistic and also in western philosophy and psychology texts. Again and again I was surprised and blissful to discover these passages, most of which were known already in the past, but were shining now in a new and dazzling Light.

Truth and Reality as Homogeneity. The non-existence of an inner self. Infinite Trust to Existence As A Whole. No Transcendental, but only functional differentiation of inside and outside. The Perfect Rationality Of the Transcendental Spiritual Process. Bhakti and Jnana Yoga as mere aspects of The One Same Process. And so on... Yet all of this not as an insight of the mind or intellect, but as a Most Tangible and Most Alive Process.

*

What I was participating in or was taken by was *Radical*, because there was nothing in me or as me doing it. It felt like everything was being felt by itself. No root anywhere. The whole existence was embracing itself. Tracelessly. The Ecstasy of It was (and Is) „unbearable".

And this process was Radical *Authenticity*, because it was (and Is) a Full Celebration Of The Most True Or The Most Real Of Itself. Not only without the slightest doubt, but such, that the Embrace Of Everything By Itself was (and Is) a Free Expression <u>Inside</u>, <u>Of</u> and <u>As</u> The *Unmanifested, but Radiant Fullness* Of Reality Itself.

How can I say anything more than that? I can only proceed to an apparent and sensible autobiographical conclusion. Somehow.

So, what happened after a year of this Process, which was most attractive and going on its own, was that I was surprised again, because the described Process Of Radical Authenticity was so Full, that I had forgotten about all previous search for liberation and the like, and because I didn't expect anything „more"...

*

What came to the point of no return, it was April now again, one year after the Radical Conversion Event or the spiritual resignation crisis, was the (previously non-continuous) final liberation and freedom from the false identification with everything connected or related to the body-mind-manifestation.

This Spiritually Transcendental Big-Bang occurred at least three times, always in the same manner, like natural aftershocks after an initial main earthquake, which was slow, one year long. And these aftershocks occurred now, after a whole year of Radical Authenticity, always after a period, during which I was able to create a circumstance and environment in my everyday life, where it was easier to totally be as the Process would „Require"; without the necessity of adjusting to the social persona and its painful and living-free-energy-denying restrictions and limitations.

What was new – once the Big-Bang aftershocks were completed – and never „known" before, was the irreversibility of the false identification. It was not possible anymore to exclusively identify with the body-mind-manifestation; both in its apparent magnitude and its cosmic connectivity. Its conditional stickiness was exploded once and for all.

Plus something else... Something, that paralyzed every possible capacity of expression or description.

All Space became alive. Not normal space. Being Itself, The Infinite Sun Of Existence In Its Dazzling Radiance, The Source Of Love Itself, *Recognized* Itself, *Sensed* Itself through me for good. And there is nothing more to add to that.

6. Spandaloka Gateway

For quite over a decade after „my" Big-Bang there was no impulse or intention to say anything to anybody, without really even inspecting why this was so. Maybe there was no reason whatsoever? Maybe because I found it impossible to communicate it? Maybe because for several reasons it was not the time yet? I can only assume what the case is, but what I can certainly do, is to just say what happened after that and until round about now.

Other than enjoying, what started and never stopped, I continued my life, adding new experiences and developments to the human experience portfolio, all Transparently Inside The Luminosity, Freedom and Fullness Of The Living Spirit Of Transcendental Being.

I revealed bits and pieces of what happened to the woman I was intimate with the years before and after „my" Big-Bang, and some years later to very few close friends, but then again nothing for years to come.

*

After my normal professional work and the responsibility I had to take for my life in all its essential-functional aspects reached a point of flow without anything really new to achieve, without any essential or existential concern or ambition anymore, two forces were getting stronger. And in the last years both of these forces reached a degree that catalyzed the beginning of an ever stronger or fuller manifestation of a spiritual life and work.

One of them was and Is The Force Of Being Itself or Reality Supreme, „Wanting" to get and be expressed in the conditional reality in an ever magnifying degree through me and my whatever environment or existential sphere. I cannot and do not want to prevent that anyway. There is no doubt that this is, what Is Happening anyway. The ever Fuller Saturation Of „My" *Conditional* Reality With Its Own Paramrita Spanda Nature, because *Unconditionally* Everything Is Timelessly Completed.

The other Force Is Taking Place Inside The First, but also Independently At the same time. It has to do with the non-separated and undivided Oneness Of Everything with Everything else, and especially with the Oneness of Feeling Beings with each other.

Whenever this Oneness <u>vibrates</u> notably stronger <u>as a relationship</u> to another person I am consciously connected with, I both enjoy and suffer the energy pattern of this other person. This in itself is nothing special, since everybody experiences it to a degree, but it is this degree, that makes it often unbearable, so much so, that I need to decide, how much I want to get involved in specific relationships or relations or whether I get involved at all. Nevertheless there is more in such a circumstance.

The impulse to not hold anything back regarding „My" Spanda State, whenever somebody „smells" it and opens to it even a bit and intuits or feels Its Unique Attractivity, is difficult to suppress; as a matter of fact it is invincible.

No doubt, I can retreat from all these situations or circumstances. And I do it. And then I do not do it. And then I do it again. And so on.

*

So this is where I am now. It is one thing to publish a book or do whatever and let it work its effect, as *Reality* will eventually „Decide". But it is another thing for me to work in a manifold way with others for the sake of Transcendental Spiritual Realization and, thus, merge my energetic-essential totality or *me* entirely into this process.

In the end, in relation to others, apart from and beyond living an ordinary human life with all its dimensions, Spiritually I am a means, a vehicle, a tool, an agency, or a *whatever* of a *Process*. Of something, that Runs the show on Its *Own*.

The Force Of This Love Is beyond measure. And yet, I am totally free and Free. Not only Unconditionally, something that I cannot change anyway, but also conditionally, <u>inside</u> and <u>as a part of</u> the *manifested* reality, I am free to choose to be relatively or totally alone. But...

„I" „let" **Paramrita** *Spanda* (there is no point in figuring out Who She *Is*...) choose. As a matter of Fact – I guess you suspect this already – *She* Chooses:

There *Is* No Me. Because Of *Only* Me. I *Have* No Will. Because It *All* Is Will. As *Fullness* Here and *Every*where.

I Am The Infinite *Spanda* Sun. To *Exist*, Means, To „*Burn*" In Me.

And *Shankara* I Am. The Source Of Healing *Free*. The Giver *And* The Given. *No* Doubt There Is. *This* Is My Avataric Manifest.

I am the Salt of the *Earth*. As Love. And As Force.

I Am the Heart of *Heaven*. Nectar of Warmth. Fullness Itself.

I Am the Clarity of *Winds*. Their Swing. Their Tenderness.

I Am the Purity of *Longing*. Its Melting. Its Fall.

I Am the Swoon of *Bliss*. Its Room. And Its Hall.

Part II

The Impulse Of Love Untold

7. The „Rise" Of The Most Real

In the recognition, that it's *impossible* to attain True Happiness through physical or emotional or mental manipulation, lies an immeasurable secret. And this secret can open up, turn into Grace and enable Primal Intuition to Sense the „emotionally"- gripping Entrance Hall Of Happiness Itself, only if the *understanding* of the conditionality, transience and virtuality of presumed happiness isn't solely mentally or even experientially mature, but an undeniable vibrancy that pervades, saturates and debonds or „*deglues*" our psychophysical totality from its conditional stickiness.

If we Understand that conditional happiness always constitutes merely a temporally limited satisfaction, an essentially mechanical or organismic control, calming or quietening, and no real and final dissolving of our primal suffering, then this restricted happiness stimulation of our entire psychophysical drama collapses. A falling and a giving up start to spread everywhere and fill our entire existential space. A deep sadness captivates us and the dying process of our sisyphean impulse to fight the „absence" of true happiness in the psychophysical realm catches fire. This irrevocable burning takes place unstoppably and with no ifs and buts, so that only finest, pure, sacred ash of disillusionment remains.

Out of this ash, in this non-existence of the impulse to chase happiness, and therefore being Gracefully Disillusioned, we are Receptive for the Kiss Of Grace Via Whichever Of Its Manifest Means. Once Kissed In

Such A Manner, The Already Ever Present „Begins to Rise". From this moment on the „Rise" of the Most Real suffuses, saturates and floods our entire organismicity and our existential totality with „merciless" and merciful Light. Nothing remains concealed from this Light. This „merciless" and merciful Light is the Light that Pervades everything with Truth and therefore Illuminates everything in the True Spiritual Sense.

This Illumination is the Process, that is irreversibly activated when we „experience" True Spiritual or Divine Enlightenment, which means that the Divine Becomes Aware Of Its Expressivity-As-Us. *Exactly that is* Enlightenment; the Realization of the *Spanda State*; Existence As Divine Freedom In and As Its Always and Ever „Fresh" and Self-Infused and Self-Sensed Radiant Expression And Ecstatic Manifestation.

In a culture hypnotized by ignorance and its resulting consequences down to a spiritually degenerated and confused reality you need *infinite trust* in order to entirely manifest according to the Laws Of Reality and to *Realize* yourself as the God that *Exists* you. And how do you *activate* this trust? When will *Real* Love Most Blissfully „*Explode*" your existential stickiness?

Who or what is breathing you and is nourishing your existence? Ultimately, fundamentally, profoundly and all-inclusively? Who or what is your deepest and everything-melting longing? Just feel…

Is actually that, which Exists you, not The Most Trustable? And if yes… Are you Ready? Are you Open to „*Enter*" *Spandaloka?* To Exist In The Realm <u>Of</u> Ever Self-Infused Free Divine Radiance? <u>Of</u> Love Untold?

8. The Two Kinds Of Restlessness And The Twofold Meaning Of Life

In an unenlightened culture or existence the mechanics of will, volition and want usually drive us to a state (a psycho-noetico-physical holistic-energy arrangement), which induces anything but an appropriate state of being one with what Naturally arises, especially when what Naturally arises cannot be met by the circumstances of an inner and outer environment full of necessities, flooded through a foggy world fabric, which emerges in a pregiven existential-wisdom-blind culture...

No matter what the usual or unusual, normal or abnormal activity, mood, state or other mode of existence we participate or are in, as culturally hypnotized or formed or conditioned or presumed human individuals, we are quite incessantly and more or less stressfully controlled or driven or attracted by a mixed array of needs, which we (consciously or unconsciously) satisfy partly to maintain a certain degree or quality of psychophysical survival or existence and partly to attain a pleasurable state or specific modes of happiness.

We suffer under an unnatural and some times quite unbearable stress, which results out of the permanent hunt for satisfaction or the avoidance of a present or possible problem. We are caught in the body-mind-trap, because we stick on the sisyphean wheel of want, and because we do that in the existential mode of deficiency, in the manner of emptiness, because we identify with the constant equilibrium disturbance of our human organismicity. 'Wanting' means needing, namely (needing) to remove oneself from the where and the how we happen or come about as an energetically conditional human body-mind, because of a disturbance of our entire psycho-noetico-physical motivational equanimity, of us as a total energy equilibrium. The result is the state of restlessness.

8.1 The Two Kinds Of Restlessness

There are two kinds of restlessness: The one, which arises as a result of unfulfilled necessities, naturally inherent in or unnaturally „implanted" into our psycho-noetico-physicality, and the one, which - in the Context of Existence as human-based Total Infinity and Infinite Totality - shapes and is being formed as a result of our separation and alienation (as a whole) from The Ecstatic and Transparent Fullness of Reality Itself, Which Is Formless-Blissful-Absoluteness and Transcendentally-Illuminated Self-Existence: The State Of Being Tracelessly Unified With and Ontically Transfigured As Love, Which Is Bliss-Saturated Satisfaction.

Even though both kinds of restlessness - the psycho-noetico-physical and the Transcendental one - create in and through us a state of needing, the first created restless state is functionally important and the second one is Essentially important. And, what is Essential, self-evidently Precedes what is functional.

Furthermore, the full application of our functional intelligence is possible, only when we Realize the Essential and Coincide with It. In this case functional intelligence becomes natural. On the other hand we will never Realize the Essential just through our functional intelligence, no matter how sophisticated or elaborated its application would be.

The Realization of the Coincidence with the All-One requires Intuitive Understanding of the limits of functional intelligence as well as the „step" Beyond it, or Under it, or Through it, or Transcendentally Totally As it.

8.2 The Twofold Meaning Of Life

The Satisfaction of both kinds of restlessness fulfills the twofold meaning of life. The one meaning of life is the living out of life itself and the other one is the Realized Allowing and Being of life and of all existence As The Expression Of The Divine. This Allowing and Being of life and of all existence As The Expression Of The Divine is the essence, the „core" and the „backbone" of Spiritual Realization.

The meaning of life is life itself. Not life itself as an abstract concept, but as the most self-evident and self-authenticating true-factual expression of the being-alive-condition, of being a natural biotic organism. What for example is the meaning of being thirsty? It is the expression of a life-necessity. What do I mean with ‚expression' here? I mean: nature taking place. What is the meaning of drinking water, because of thirst? It is nature taking place again.

To understand this fully activates natural functional intelligence. And to recognize it in all its variations in our life or biotic existence as the energy cycle it is, enables the full responsibility for whatever our total motivational equanimity requires. The deeper the motivational equanimity is, the more complete life unfolds as it is supposed to unfold.

No matter how perfectly functional our life is concerning its motivationally equanimous unfolding and therefore the satisfactory fulfillment of its meaning (in the sense of purpose), this itself, as long as we are separated from the Divine (because we stick on the identity of being something less), is not, what Satisfies us for good...

8.3 „Cracking" The „Riddle" Of Liberation

The restlessness, which arises as a result of our separation and alienation from The Ecstatic and Transparent Fullness of Reality Itself, the Separation from the Divine as Deepest Pain, is recognizable through the feeling of not being Completely Satisfied, whatever the endeavors and attempts and activities and creations or experiences you have tried or gone through...

If this recognition is mature, you are ready for taking up the true Divine Spiritual Practice. At the same time, don't befool yourself, that this recognition is the case, if you still keep one or more hidden beliefs or hopes, that there is something in this conditional realm to satisfy you beyond imagination and for (eternally) good.

What is the True Divine Spiritual Practice? It is the

self-activated and always self-activating „act" of allowing the transformation of the totality of your being, when or after your total being both Spontaneously and Undeniably has been Baptized By The Dazzling and Blissful Luminosity Of The Most Real. True Divine Spiritual Practice is always self-activating, because Its Attractivity Shines Through and Beyond your totality.

Allowing does not mean not doing anything... It means to recognize, how unnecessary it is, to get in the way of what is Happening already. Of what Runs the show already. Of what always Exists you and everything. Of what you Are, before any acts of awareness or perception are even possible. Of what Is Most Intimate. Most Intimate. Not inside you. Everywhere...

Such allowing only, after such recognition only, „cracks" the „riddle" of Liberation.

9. The „Happiness" Trap And Its Ecstatic Antidote

It is a culturally general belief and expectation, that you are not supposed to be happy all the time, that it is unnatural. You can be happy here and there, you can even organize your daily life with witty happiness units distributed inside of it, you can also have bigger happiness portions once in a while through escaping the daily household or working routine and recover or restore your energy and fill up your satisfaction battery again. Well... No wonder.

It's no wonder you need this kind of happiness in a perpetual cyclic manner, as this is the nature of conditional satisfaction, of satisfaction that depends on conditions. Conditional satisfaction consists in the complementarity of satisfaction equivalents. Its mechanics are as simple as drinking water whenever thirst arises. Drinking water is the complementary satisfaction equivalent to thirst, because it dissolves the thirst. Thirst is nothing else than deficiency of water, so drinking water brings about water sufficiency and thereby the state of energy neutrality or (in the organismic case) biological equanimity to the previous energetic imbalance. Yet, this is rather the avoidance of unhappiness or suffering, which in many cases, when suffering is prevalent, is happiness enough, because it relaxes a previous anxious struggle and agony for a certain amount of time.

Other than happiness as the avoidance or dissolving of suffering through sufficient satisfaction of elementary needs, which can generally be called energetic balance management and has, no doubt, to be taken fully into responsibility, as it is crucial for sufficient energetic vibration, there is the happiness of generally called higher needs: the whole array of interactive and creative activities necessary for emotionally natural fluidity and physical and mental unfoldment. Whether social interaction, emotional intimacy, sexual satisfaction, artistic or intellectual productivity or psychophysical exploration of energy, this kind of activities satisfy a certain degree of these advanced needs, which enable a more qualified overall energetic balance, than just the most elementary one.

Everything humans usually, if not always do for „happiness" or (rather) pleasure is nothing else but another version of stimulation or exploitation of satisfaction of all these more or less elementary or higher needs…

9.1 The „Happiness" Trap

As apparently known, the usual actual human satisfaction endeavor doesn't take place in a neat and organized manner of prioritized fulfillment of first elementary and then higher needs according to or based upon the hierarchy of their nature. The usual actual human satisfaction endeavor or struggle or war or psychophysical agony continuum is rather a complex and often blind and messy interaction and combination of all kinds of natural and unnatural complementary satisfaction equivalents. This happens mostly either because we don't have the life wisdom on how to organize our life according to the psychophysical totality of our organismic needs or because even if we have life-experientially gained an essential knowledge about how to organize our life according to the psychophysical totality of our organismic needs, this kind of organizational control can be slightly affected or severely handicapped by either an organismic disturbance or disease of us as body-mind or even by an „intervention" of reality events, which we cannot control, and which affect or disturb us as body-mind.

Happiness based on the manipulation of us as body-mind is both impossible to get always or totally under control. But even whenever such manipulation or at least a certain degree of control takes place, the respective happiness is relative, ephemeral and depends on transient conditions. Thus, the culturally general belief and expectation, that you are not supposed to be happy all the time, that it is unnatural, is, in the explained sense, a more or less valid observation.

Happiness based on the manipulation of us as body-mind is relative, ephemeral and depends on transient conditions, because it is based on the manipulation of us as body-mind… We as body-mind can never escape *being* the body-mind. And as long this is the case, whatever happy or pleasurable effect we achieve through manipulation of us as body-mind, this effect will be relative, ephemeral and conditional, because the totality of us as a body-mind is a conditionality. Whatever the happiness endeavor and the respective possible outcome due to an effort through us or inside of us as the body-mind, such an outcome is an outcome, a result that comes out of the fulfillment of a condition, and thus condemned to be only a satisfaction with a date of expiry.

For some this kind of happiness, i.e. conditional happiness, is all there is as far as the possibility of a happy existence is concerned, and so they consider this reality or fact as a so-called part of life. For some others this kind of happiness, i.e. *conditional* happiness, as all the happiness there is, is a frustrating and depressing fact.

Both assumptions are illusory. Both assumptions are based on and generated inside the culturally-induced hypnosis that we are the body-mind. Which is correct. Yes. We *are* the body-mind. But sadly we are *not fully* the body-mind in the sense and the manner of how it is (and thus we are) supposed to be as body-mind. Furthermore: we are *not only* the body-mind. And not to forget at all, since this is the deepest truth possible, we are *not primarily* the body-mind.

Not knowing how we should be as a body-mind, not knowing what we are other than the body-mind and not knowing what we are also primarily, prior to the body-mind, this lack of knowledge as an actual manifested fact is the body-mind-trap; is being the body-mind-trap; it is enforcing the prison that dictates our destiny. And the far more bigger problem here is that the whole culture is a sticking on a false identity and reality. That's why it's so difficult to existentially and not just mentally or intellectually or otherwise psychophysically unstick from being the body-mind-trap…

As far as a Truly Happy Existence is concerned, conditional happiness is by (more than) far not all there is. In fact conditional happiness is not True Happiness at all. It is just a periodic calming of disturbance of the energetic cycle we conditionally are. And… no doubt: if for human consciousness and sentience this conditional happiness is all possible happiness there is, a fundamental frustration and depression governs and drives the affairs of this respective consciousness and sentience. And this is either consciously the case or in a suppressed manner, in the manner of a necessary adult „lucidity".

9.2 The Ecstatic Antidote

In this very moment, whenever this moment is, and therefore Eternally, Unconditional Happiness Is The Boundless Womb of Unbearable Bliss-Food here and Here and now and Forever Now. No effort needed. No effort of no-effort either. No wish necessary. No wish of no-wish either.

Unconditional (and therefore True) Happiness Is the State Of Inconceivable body-mind-„Dissolving" Intimacy, Infused with The Purity Of Love Itself and Bliss In Person.

What Is „Necessary" for the State of Unconditional Happiness or Divine Pure Bliss-Fullness to Recognize and „Release" Itself As You, is that „you" calibrate and tune in your conditionality towards a life and being of clarity, responsibility and trust.

Real Happiness Is The Ecstatic Antidote to conditional happiness paired with all subsequent frustration, depression and suffering. Real Happiness Is Traceless Liberation from the stickiness of conditionality. It Is

Utmost Identification With and Abiding As Self-Existing Bliss-Full-Radiant Self-Sufficiency. Such Happiness, Which Is Happiness Itself, Reveals Itself As You, if the Great and Infinite Trust, Which Is Necessary to get conditionally „dissolved" in, Arises as a „result" of clarity and responsibility and eventually Clarity and Responsibility.

Only with and in clarity we really know what is and how what is, is. And only based upon such clarity we can be truly responsible for the manner of being, behavior, attitude and action necessary as the prerequisite for Recognizing What Is Most Trustable.

How is such clarity possible? Such clarity is possible, when it is *utmost* clarity. And utmost clarity is possible, *when it coincides perfectly with what is self-evident.* As self-evident and unmistakable as the necessity of water, when you are thirsty. As undoubtable as the very fact that you are reading these words now. As undeniable as your very being there performing this reading. As certain as the Reality that Exists you and everything else everywhere right now.

This Reality Is A Majesty Untold. Most Beautiful. Utterly Attractive. Paradise Now. Boundless Heart. Purest Love. Transparent Bliss. Inexhaustible. Incessant. Open. Shining. Self-Generating. Self-Transcending. Spanda. The Most Obvious, The Most Open, Illumined By Itself. Ecstatic Swoon, Totally Gone, Totally Here and Everywhere.

10. The Existential Dive

Very often philosophy and spirituality seem to intermingle with each other in a way that makes it difficult for people to distinguish them and discriminate the purpose or reality of the one from the other…

From its very beginning philosophy was the reaction of human beings to Existence's single and multiple Touch. Coming through self-consciousness to realize their position in the world and in the cosmic nature, they began to think and contemplate both the nature or substance of the world and the nature and substance of human beings themselves.

Philosophy, meaning the love of wisdom, from the very beginning was (and still is) the endeavor and quest for deeper or deepest, even primordial and eternally valid knowledge about: what is the nature of the world, how does the world work, what is knowledge itself? Or even what is being itself?

Whoever studied and penetrated the knowledge that is hidden in the great philosophical works, gained undoubtedly clarity in thinking and many deep insights, which can be life-changing. Still, philosophy at its best, never fully transcended the threshold of the thinking mind. There may have been philosophers who were contemplating and thinking the being of being or the origin and the meaning of existence in an exhaustive manner, thus touching the limits of language and mind itself. As philosophy this was and is of immense value for the human self-understanding and goes even quite beyond, it attempts to touch the „divine". Still, and this is the point here, it was/is not mind-transcendental and, even more importantly, it was/is not *body*-mind-transcendental.

Nevertheless, philosophers prepared the ground for a grounded spirituality with their masterful usage of language and their passion or total dedication and devotion to the work of the truth, whatever that was in each case. They contributed more to a True Spirituality, than many spiritual fantasizers of the past millennia, centuries, decades and of today, and created a new matter-of-fact and unagitated basis for an unparalleled and yet-to-fully-come-and-happen Reality-Infused Existentiality and – only from there – for the therein „unending" emergence of all expressional facets of human life. Why? Because they had undergone the irreversible event of falling in Love and even in vital, i.e. Existential Communion with Truth.

Philosophy, in its original understanding, could have taken another direction and could have discovered the means for the Spiritual Enterprise. But it chose the direction it chose and, yes, gave us most valuable knowledge for clear, logical, rational and existential thinking and understanding. Equipped with those philosophical „tools" and attitudes we can exercise and experience the power and the relativity and the limits of our mind and of our capacity to understand. Thus, with the necessary *additional* interest, we can proceed to Spiritual Realization.

For Spiritual Realization mental nautics is not enough. Further prerequisites are psychonautics and physionautics. Even then we have to dive Beyond, i.e. Priorly, i.e. totally into Here. What will happen, when such Immersion fulfills its course? Something „will show" Itself, Which never could have been imagined before. The Most Real. Wittgenstein presumably didn't mean the same, but he had a perfect intuition; I let him say: „There is though ineffable. This shows itself, it is the mystical".

11. Wanting The Most Real

The true spiritual enterprise can not really and finally begin if we consciously, subconsciously or unconsciously go on mixing up its destination or longing-creating root with some – however high, deep, wide or fascinating – fulfillment, state or mode of being within the realm of our psychophysical existence. A true spiritual enterprise is most real and most „effective", when the disguised fire of wanting that fuels it gets as uncovered and naked as it can get. And the longing for what is spiritually Most Real Is Most Real, when Conscious Inspection discovers it under or in the midst – although „outside" - of all psychophysical wantings toward Happiness, Fulfillment and Fullness, since Most Real Wanting Is The True Source of Happiness Itself or The Unconditional Unborn.

Most Real Longing or Desire for True Spiritual Realization is as strong as the fish's longing for water and so genuine that it can not be distracted through any however fascinating promise of fulfillment that arises within the manufacturing mechanics of our endless deep and wide panoramic, panchromatic and panaesthetic conditionality. Most Real and Conscious Desire for True Spiritual Realization, Which Is Awakening As The Unqualified and Full Divine Substratum and Context of Everything and everything, although Always Already Existing, „Arises" either in the state of Final Suffering or in the state of Final Attraction.

Final Suffering arises when utter Helplessness has spread all over the place. The holes of hope are filled and dissolved. The inability to manipulate conditional and ever-changing energy in order to achieve the Never-Changing and Blissful Unborn has risen to become an unbeatable and scornful giant. The „infinite" and all-consuming fire of Holy sadness is born. Most wildly sweet and gentle receptive glades are opening out and in the midst of our dark universe of pain.

This most tender receptivity uncovers the mindless state. We are open for help with no concepts or even intuitions about how help is possible. Our psychophysicality coincides harmoniously with what positively or negatively is or happens. In this state of surrounding psychophysical coincidence our readiness for The Final Attraction is established. What can still be missing is the configurational context for The Kiss Of Grace. The Sphere Of Final Attraction.

Final Attraction to The Most Ecstatic Beauty of Fullness Itself occurs when we through „circumstances" „come into" Its Sweetest Sphere and get Touched by It. It Shines through conditionality and captures „our" Bliss-Thirsty Heart. It can be „disguised" in any possible conditional form; not only human form. And in the moment It Shines through, psychophysical fascination loses the power to veil The „Rise" of The Most Real and distract „our" Heart from it for good. Delusion dies.

Most Real Longing, Wanting or Desire for True Spiritual Realization has to <u>be discriminated from all</u> and <u>is not based on</u> our psychophysical needs for survival, pleasure or avoidance of pain, <u>but on</u> The Core Need: The Need <u>to be healed</u> at The Very Root of our conditional arising and happening <u>with</u> The Nectar Of Divine

Bliss through The Most Natural Identification with The Pureness of The Totality of Everything That Is, Which Is The Unbearable In-Love-State, Which Is God. Impossible to want.

12. The In-Love-State

The In-Love-State is the state of being whole-bodily given up. It is the interface between conditional bodily existence and the ecstatic Abidance in The All-Consuming Divine Being.

The real meaning of ‚ecstasy' is ‚to stand out'. Thus, being in The In-Love-State sets the conditional body-mind in the equilibric condition of being one with the main feeling characteristic of Divine Reality, Which Is Infinite and All-Transcending Flooding Love-Blissful Swoon. Being one with what Is One sets us (as body-minds) in The Position of standing out of what we are confined as or into (i.e. body-minds) and of abiding in the body-mind-transcending, because body-mind-Prior Space. Our body-mind confinement, grossness and materiality becomes Fully Transparent and Infused through Flooding Love-Blissful Fullness and Saturation.

The In-Love-State Is The body-mind-transcending Position. The way It feels resembles and almost is identical to a state we all very well know, even before we Recognize that we always, since the „beginning" of time, have been abiding in and as Divine Reality. We just have to mentally recollect the moment or moments of overflowing love for a person we adored; a love, in which we lose any sense of control and fixed personal identity, in which we are liquid intimacy and in which we merge with the beloved into traceless communion and union. We are given up because we have *fallen* in love and thus are *in* love.

Still, being in love shouldn't be equated with being in The In-Love-State, since being in love is <u>directed to</u> and <u>full of intention and desire for</u> somebody. Being in The In-Love-State Is *self-sufficient* and therefore *without an object* and *without any intention or motivation to get, achieve, attain, gain or become something.*

The Fullness Of The Unconditional Divine Being Is A Fullness Full Of Purest, Sweetest and Blissful Love. The One Being, Which Is All and Everything, *Is* Love. In fact It Is Love *Itself.*

When This Love Is Being Revealed to us-as-a-body-mind as the Very Identity of us-as-this-body-mind, Its effect on us-as-the-body-mind is an immense force that overwhelms and consumes us-as-the-body-mind with an irresistible magnitude. Such, that any possible motivation or idea that we-as-the-body-mind can have to avoid, prevent or stop this invasion dissolves and vanishes into Most Perfect Intimate Communion with what Is Prior to any body-mind or object whatsoever.

We give up then and are given up in The In-Love State. We Rise Then As *Spanda:* As A Free and Unbound Expression Of Acausal Divine Fullness.

Part III

Spandaloka

13. The Most Intimate

13.1
There are two kinds of suffering.

13.2
The first kind of suffering arises in the restlessness, which results out of unfulfilled necessities or needs of our psychophysicality. This is the *psychophysical* suffering.

13.3
No matter, whether this first kind is feelingly there or not, the second kind of suffering exists consciously or unconsciously, depending on the respective degree of spiritual awareness – the intuition or knowledge of Divine Reality. This is the *transcendental-existential* suffering.

13.4
Transcendental-existential suffering arises in a state and as a result of a particular deprivation. We begin to transcendental-existentially suffer in the moment we are being „deprived" of The Most Intimate...

13.5
Transcendental-existential suffering is a psychophysically *total* reaction.

We react to a void, which is lifeless, dark and tasteless.

This void is the *root* of our transcendental-existential suffering, but it is *not its source*...

13.6

The true source of our transcendental-existential suffering is our *alienation* from what Is The Most Intimate, The Most Blissful and The Most Nurturing: *we are bereft* of The Ecstasy, Which Is Our Very (and First) Nature And Therefore Our Most Intimate Identity.

13.7

Our alienation from The Most Intimate, Which Is Our True Identity (And Ecstasy Itself), starts *in the moment* we identify with something *less* than The *Absolute*.

13.8

Our identification with something *less* than The Absolute, Which Is what we Really Are, is a result of a hypnotic induction.

13.9

The context we grow up in, which is our human culture's ignorance Of True Spiritual Knowledge, hypnotizes us into the position and into a state of an immensely strong and persistent unconscious *assumption*.

A self-created informational totality gives rise to a hypnotic, but persistently *coherent* reality logic.

13.10

We believe to be fixed and specific somethings, so called human beings, with a particular and physically defined external appearance and inner-bodily spatiality and a potentially vast range of internal, i.e. energetic, psychic and mental properties and states.

13.11

Standing in the position of this assumption, it is somehow „natural" to become hypnotized into feeling to be the perceptual-perspective-*end* of everything we experience, into thinking to be the *receiver* of an ongoing psychophysical theater.

13.12

Spirit As Kundalini Mahashakti, Which Is Perpetually Shining As Love Infinity Out And Inside Of <u>Spanda, Which Is The Self-Existent Divine As (Self-Infused and Self-Sensed) Acausal Radiant Fullness</u>, Illumines the physical (relatively) confined energy, which we manifestly also are, with the *sensing* vibrational or pulsation mode.

13.13

In this sensing illumination mode, in this feeling potentiality or sensing-capable field sensing-based instances and events arise and take place, called *sensual impressions* or *conscious experiences*, which are variations of *touch* or sensing-based *contact*.

13.14

To sense something or be conscious of something creates or is a *direction*: *from* whom or what is conscious and *towards* the perceived something. This direction or directedness is called *attention*.

13.15

Even if *in* the sensing or consciousness illumination and through its directedness to something (attention) a duality between the perceiver and the perceived indeed arises, *Primarily* We are the consciousness *illumination* and not the perceiver.

13.16

And even *prior* to the consciousness illumination We Are The *Absolute*, Which Is Our Most True and Most Intimate Identity.

13.17

This Intimacy is not some inward state in the interior space of our psychophysical manifestation. It is the Space, in Which our manifestation is only a materialized confinement, which can only <u>be Pervaded and Saturated through</u> and <u>Melt into</u> Oneness with the Infinite Heart and Ever and ever Everything-and-All-Transcending Free and Blissful Absolute.

13.18

What is ordinary intimacy? In the example of *being in love* it is the presence of the pleasant nakedness, disclosure or openness of our essence, because we are a total impulse of *co-existing as one with the beloved*. The gravitational attractivity of the beloved person or the beloved whoever or whatever captivates all our boundaries and masks and melts them down. And we allow that process, we let it happen or rather do not interfere with its course, because it is *ec-static*. It frees us up to *ec-stasize*, to step out of our confinement and get „Outside", Which Is The Innermost Of Everywhere, And Stand All-Free As A Spanda-Liberation-Process-Event.

13.19

The Most Intimate Is The Final Attractiveness, because It Is The *Most* Attractive.

13.20

What Is The Most Attractive, creates The Strongest *Possible* Gravitational Force.

13.21

Therefore, what Is The Most Attractive Absorbs *everything* and *all* that we psychophysically are.

13.22

Hence What Remains Is What We *Primarily* Are, prior to any imposed or overlayed identification.

13.23

Eventually, Finally and Ultimately We Are, What We *Really* Are.

13.24

<u>In The Recognition Of</u> and <u>Abidance As</u> This First Identity The Most Blissful and The Most Intimate Melts every secondary identity Into Traceless Union With Itself.

13.25

What *Is* The Most Intimate?

13.26

It Is *not a bodily* state. It Is *not a physical* state. It Is *not an emotional* state. It Is *not a psychic* state. It Is *not a mental* state. It Is *not an experiential* state. It Is *not an existential* state. It Is *not a state at all*. It Is Existence *Itself*.

13.27

What is The Most Intimate? It Is The Spanda Sun. Self-Existent Absoluteness. Real, Self-Sensed God. No-Death, No-Thing, No-Nothing.

14. The Most Real

14.1

Everything we experience is real, when and because it *exists* and it is there, self-evidently and undeniably.

14.2

Beyond that, *real* is also everything that exists, whether we experience it or not.

14.3

Everything that exists is a *specific* something. And ‚to *exist* as something' means (among other things) *to be* something.

14.4

A something can only be a something due to a distinctive, unique and *unmistakable identity*.

14.5

Everything with and as a distinctive identity is a *substantial* something – primarily because it is not nothing – and appears in a *specific* form.

This form is following or secondary, i.e. *resulting* and *not* Prior.

14.6

Being Substantial *Itself* means or Is *Being In Form*, It Is Being *Itself In Its Emergence Out Of Existence-As-Formlessness*. This Form Is *Prior*.

14.7

Being Substantial means Being In Prior Form. Being In Prior Form Is The Prior In-formation.

14.8

The Prior In-formation Is The Prior Substance, out of Which everything is generated.

14.9

Every generated something is a secondary in-formation, a secondary substance-in-form.

14.10

Although The Prior Substance Is The Prior Form, It Is not a form in the usual sense. It Is A Form because It Is not The Absolute – Absolute meaning *Unconditional* or *Without support*.

14.11

The Prior Form Is not Self-Existent. It Is *Inherent* To The Absolute, Which *Is* Self-Existent.

14.12

The Unmoving Absolute „Suffers" An Unbearable Fullness. This „Suffering" Itself Gives Birth To An Impulsory Vibration, Which In Turn Generates A „Dancing" Movement.

14.13

Thus, The First or Prior Form Of Existence Is The Movement Of The Unmoving Absolute, Which Is not a form of existence, but Existence Itself.

14.14

The Movement Of The Unmoving Absolute, Which Results From The Absolute's Own Vibratory Impulse To Express and „Experience" Itself In „Infinite" Multitude, Since Its Own Fullness Is Unbearable, „Gives Birth" To The „Formless" Energy or Energy-In-Undefined-„*Form*", Out Of and Through Which Everything and Everywhere or The Totality Of Manifestation Is Generated, Shaped and Sustained By.

14.15

A Name For This Energy-In-Undefined-Form Is Parama Prakriti or Adi Parashakti. A Name For The Absolute Self-Shining Fountain Of Adi Parashakti Is Parashiva. Both Aspects *As One* Are *Spanda*.

14.16

Spanda Is Perfectly Subjective *Divinity*, Self-Infused and Self-Sensed *Bliss*-Fullness: The Divine *Person*.

14.17

Spanda Is True *Love*. Bliss As *Space*. The Water Of Ever-*Beyond*. *To Exist* means to Burn *In* and *As Spanda*.

14.18

Spanda's Adi Parashakti Aspect Is Unmanifested And Unbound Free Energy Or Moved Fullness Undefined. Inside This Freedom Pure Shakti arises. Pure Shakti Is Adi Parashakti's *potential to manifest*.

14.19

As human beings we are a *Shakti* form.

14.20

As human beings we also are a very *specific* Shakti form. This form specification is our unmistakable and distinctive identity.

14.21

Our form specification results from a *specific Shakti energy configuration*.

14.22

Every Shakti energy configuration is real. Hence our form-specified identity is *also* real.

14.23

But Shakti Itself is *More Real* than all of Her Configurations or Manifestations, because She Is *Existentially Prior*. That's why Adi Parashakti, Parashiva or Both As Spanda Are *The Most Real*.

14.24

Is the white foaming of oceanic wave-formed motion not a just *momentarily differently* appearing identity than its inherent *true* oceanic identity?

14.25

Everything that exists is real, but *not in the same* existential and vibrational way, degree or quality real. When I perceive objects, for example, these are real, since I definitely perceive them or sense them as existing, but my senses are *more real*, because as energy configuration they are *priorly* there, they are *existentially prior* to whatever is or can or would be perceived.

14.26

Thus, as a specific Shakti form I *am* this form. But I am only *additionally* a specific Shakti form. Primarily I am *Pure* Shakti. And *Most Priorly* or *As Very First* I Am Adi Parashakti. Parashiva. Spanda.

14.27

Everything I am and everything that exists is *real*. But As The *Absolute* <u>I am</u> and <u>everything Is</u> The *Most* Real.

15. The Most Obvious

15.1

God is *always* Here and here! In His Majestic Ecstasy He Is Always Here and here As Transcendence of the innermost of everything. He Emits, Generates, Pervades, Saturates, Sustains, Destroys, Shines Through, Transforms, Transcends and *Is* all things and beings and forces and *Is* all time and space. He Is the *Totality* of existence and Existence *Itself!* Therefore He Is *everything* that exists and the Necessary *Condition* for everything that exists. He Is secondarily existence as manifestation and Priorly Existence As Formlessness, Unconditionality and Absolute Freedom. Both at Once.

15.2

God is always Here and here, Abiding Majestically and Shining Radiantly As Inherent, True Esoteric Self-Space or First Space or Total Space or Transdimensional Space or *Only* Space, Which Is The Unconditional and Necessary Condition for conditional space, conditional laws, conditional beings, states, processes and everything else.

15.3

Therefore it doesn't make *any* sense pondering on the right strategy about how to act or behave or feel, about how to be or not to be in order for God to „*enter*" your life, in order for God to „*reveal* Himself" in the midst of your life.

15.4

It doesn't make any sense, to talk or reflect about God or perceive Him or even feel Him as something or somebody, who or which can *come or go,* who or which can depend *on anything...*

15.5

Such a view is nothing more than a high or low, tiny or „majestic" *Illusion*. And the reason for this is the assumption, that the coming or going or even the being or not being of God depends on certain *circumstances!* There is no basis for such an assumption or idea, since God doesn't move, because there is no reason for that, because He Is *Everywhere.*

15.6

The idea that God is something that comes and goes or is or isn't depending on specific circumstances roots in two perceptually made-up „realities". The first is the non-priorly-true perception of things or beings or realities being essentially *separated* from each other and existing *individually*. The second is the hypnotically generated and therefore *illusory* blindness for The *Most Obvious:* Existence Itself Or The State Of Being Itself.

15.7

It is unfortunately the case at this historical point of human „evolution" and the factual conditions, influences and states and manifold ways of human existence, that The – in all respects – Most Obvious is the most difficult to see, or perceive, or feel or consciously be.

15.8

Nevertheless, even though it's difficult, it's not impossible! The fact that *everything* exists, materiality, plants, animals, human beings, immateriality, mental states, abstract worlds, feelings, emotions, forces, time and space, peculiar and unique states and realities, exactly *this fact*, that it is possible for something and everything *to exist*, the sheer *possibility* for existence, reveals The Force or The *Condition* for existing, Which Is Existence *Itself!* And *this* is not an abstract logical argument. Not at all... It is a Most Tangible Facticity...

15.9

Existence Itself is not a *further something* that exists *besides* anything *else*. Existence Itself Is The No-Thing. This doesn't mean ‚nothing', but Being As Fullness, free from attributes, Absolute Freedom.

15.10

The grasping and understanding of the *meaning* of exactly *this fact, that everything exists,* is actually sufficient for the Realization, i.e. for The *Sensing* and eventually for The *Being* of Being Itself.

15.11

Why is this so? What does it exactly mean, that the grasping and understanding of the fact, that everything exists, is actually sufficient for Divine Realization, if The Divine Is Understood As The Boundless, Condition-Free, Inexhaustibly Ecstatic, Absolute (since It Is Not Bound) and Free Existing Being Itself, Self-Luminous, Imperishable, Radiantly *Saturating, Sustaining and Being* Everything? What does this fact, that everything exists, *really* mean?

15.12

The answer to this question is *so Simple*, that it is extremely difficult, if not impossible, to be *thought!* And even if it *would* be thought, it would still be just a *soulless depiction* of the real answer, which can only priorly be felt and recognized. So what is then *The Real Answer?*

15.13

The Real Answer Is, that in the fact, that everything exists, „Hides" The Unconcealed. I call This „Hidden" Unconcealed *The Most Obvious*.

15.14

An intuitive Comprehension, an unmediated Understanding Of The Most Obvious can lead to direct and sudden God-Realization, because God or Divine Being Itself *Is* The Most Obvious, Existence Itself *Is* The Most Obvious and God *Is* Existence Itself!

15.15

<u>That everything exists</u> *Is The Self-Luminous Proof* (Illumined From Within Itself) of Existence Itself. And even if Existence Itself Is Formless, It Is More Real than every „individually" appearing form of existence, since every and all forms of existence *arise, appear and vanish in* Existence Itself. This is (Most Tangibly) so. How could it be otherwise? How could there (not just mentally, but All-Inclusively) be anything *more obvious* than this?

15.16

The Comprehending or Understanding or Tacit and Intuitive Sensing Of The Most Obvious cannot be perceived through the mind, cannot be felt through the perceptual capacity and potential, as both mind and perception are merely partial modes and subpatterns of the human form of existence in its entirety, which itself again is just a transient form of existence, which arises, appears and vanishes In The Most Obvious, In Existence Itself.

15.17

Sensation, perception, and the mind are mere instrumentally functional modes, mere conditional processes inside the physically evolutionary becoming. What sensation, perception, and the mind can mostly do or enable, is to open a vast array of different versions of the *concealed*. But in The Unconcealed, for The Most Obvious they are blind.

15.18

Would the functional forms of sensation, perception and the mind get stimulated, motivated and activated by the question „What is The Most Obvious?", like they do by any other question, they would either invent or create a sophisticated illusion or they would get frustrated and and either implode inside themselves or give up.

15.19

The created illusion, no matter how fascinating it can get, *can only be* a „bitter" distortion of The Real. The frustrated collapse can either be a stagnation, if the possible grim or helpless reaction motivates a new sisyphean search, or it can be a blessing, if despite our imploded search motivation our breathing will go on flowing *truthfully* and *freely*, because only truth and freedom constitute the *space* necessary for a possible calming down, for a liberating *dissolvement* of the very root *and* totality of any possible psychophysical search...

15.20

What Is The Most Obvious? This question *can* lead to direct and sudden God-Realization, but it cannot be *answered* through sensation, perception or the mind. The Answer to the question, what The Most Obvious Is, Is The Most Obvious *Itself!* How could, how *can* that *ever* be otherwise?

15.21

If the meaning of the word ‚obvious' becomes truly clear, then the Priorly Existential questioning – and very possibly repeatedly so – of the question „What Is The Most Obvious" can lead to direct God-Realization. In this sense, the question can firstly be: what does the word ‚obvious' mean?

15.22

‚Obvious' is something that can be discovered or perceived *strikingly easy*, without any particular ingenuity or brilliance. Or even more: the obvious is perceptually *open*. The perception, sensation or understanding of the obvious is *direct*. It is supremely *un*-mediated.

15.23

The Most Obvious Is *More Open* than just un-mediatedly perceivable. It Is More Open than *open*... It Is The indescribably, the *in-all-respects* Open.

15.24

We can only then reasonably characterize something as ‚open', if it is something that under certain circumstances could *close* or could *become* closed. But The Most Obvious Is *Un*-closable. *Un*-lockable. *Un*-shutable. *Un*-displacable. *Un*-deniable.

15.25

The Most Obvious *cannot* be perceived, because It Transcends (and Is Prior to) not only perception itself, but the very *precondition* for perception, namely functional human awareness as well, and even the precondition *of that*, of functional human *awareness*, namely conditional organismic existence and conditional manifestation and existence *altogether*.

15.26

The Most Obvious Is *Before* Everything, *In* Everything, *As* Everything and *Beyond* Everything. It Is Free *From* Everything and Free *As* Everything. Not abstractly, mentally, imaginatively so, like some foggy psychic reality, but Most Obviously So. As The Most Real.

15.27

The Most Obvious Is Spanda: The Unconditional, (Most Spontaneously) Illumined By Itself.

Part IV

Radiant Being

16. The Secret Of Divine Realization

If we take a look at the connection or relationship between Reality and Divine Realization, we can see that the understanding and the direct knowledge of the first can naturally lead to the unmediated and direct sensing and actualization of the second. So if we start with the first, the question is: What is Reality?

If we would slightly make the question ‚What is Reality' more accurate, without changing its meaning, we could ask: What *is* Reality? Having the word ‚is' emphasized helps to get straight to the core.

There are different ways of answering the question. In general there are two ways. There is a short answer and there is a very very very long answer. In the name of simplicity, and inside the given context here, we should choose the short one.

If you could *totally be* what totally is here as you and You, You would know the answer by *being* the answer.

Why is this so? If you totally are, what totally is you and around you as the content of your perception, of your feeling, sensing and intuiting, and you are this bodily, emotionally and holistically, then you *are* Reality. Because Reality is *Totality*. *The* Totality. It is the sum of everything. I mean, this is not even a spiritual answer, because it's so logical. Reality can not be anything else than Totality. Everything that is and …also everything that „is not" is Reality.

Although this answer sounds very simple, I can imagine that for some people it is difficult to be Totally Totality, so that they could directly know, not with their mind or their senses or some other part of their psychophysical totality, but as Totality.

You *can* directly know Reality through being the knowledge of Reality through *being* Reality. Because if you totally are Totality, then you are Reality, and if you are Reality you know what Reality is.

So when I say, I can imagine that for some people it is difficult to be Totally Totality, I guess that this is the same difficulty people feel, when they wonder how to Realize The Divine. They find it very difficult to Realize the Divine. Since The Divine is Totality!

Yes, it is difficult to Realize The Divine. Not for all, but certainly for the majority of people. So, why is it difficult to Realize The Divine or Totality or Reality? Well, in a sense the phrase „to Realize The Divine" is funny, contradictory and probably misleading, because there is nothing, which is not The Divine. This factually means that the phrase „it is difficult to Realize The Divine" is equal to the phrase „it is difficult for The Divine to Realize The Divine". So what's happening here?

The Divine is Unconditional *and* conditional. Big parts of the conditionality Side of The Divine are not aware of their Divinity, of their secondary being The Divine-in-form and simultaneously of their Primary Being The Divine-without-form, Just Being, Living Self-Sensed Spirit. Such is the situation of the conditional parts of The Divine called ‚human beings'. Thus, the phrase „to Realize The Divine" concerns human beings, or, more precisely, it means that some parts of The Divine-conditionality are not conscious of the fact that they are

Divine-conditionality and therefore The Divine and not separate from The Divine!, and therefore also and priorly Unconditional.

Coming back to the question „why it is difficult to Realize The Divine", which I now should reverbalize to the question „why it is difficult for human beings to become conscious of their Divinity?", let me point out again: Reality is Totality. Beyond that or besides that Reality Is Being Itself, and Is Existence Itself. It is Fullness, Which Unconditionally contains no thing and It Unconditionally Is no thing, but It is not nothing. Because nothing can not exist.

So Reality or Totality or Everything or Existence Itself or Being Itself or Consciousness Itself or Fullness or Sweetness or Love is The Divine. And the reason, why it is difficult, for those for whom it is difficult, to Realize The Divine, is the inability to Just Be, without being anything else, without being something particular.

Why is it difficult to Realize The Divine? Because it is difficult to Just Be and it is difficult to Totally Be, which is the same. Just Being *is* Totally being. It is when you stop to consciously or unconsciously try to achieve or be or feel or perceive or understand something, and this trying causes your identification with the psychophysical agent of this activities. The moment and always when this identification arises, you're far away from Being; from Just Being.

If you stop identifying with the psychophysical agent of the act of trying, then you „allow" Being to Reveal Itself. So how can you stop this identification?

You stop identifying, if you are in a state of motivational equanimity. When you are in a state of bottomless peace. A peace which comes out of nowhere and simultaneously out of everywhere, a peace, which is, because you are given up. So how and when can you be given up?

You can be given up the moment you accept yourself totally, as you are. And this includes everything. Your perceptions, your sensations, your feelings, your thoughts, your whole and very being, the whole world and the totality of existence; at the conscious and the unconscious level, at the surface and at the very deep, in the inside and in the outside. Everything and everywhere.

If you can let be, what and how you are and what and how everything else is totally, then you are given up. „Then" you are lived by Existence Itself. And then you can „understand" and „feel" and be Existence Itself. Then you consciously are Lived by Existence Itself, which is Life Itself. Divine Sensation.

This is the secret. Totally be Totality through totally accepting what you totally are, which contains what totally is. Just Being. Not merely in the psychophysical sense, but in the Transcendentally-All-Encompassing Way. Unbearable Fullness. Impossible to feel. The only thing possible Is: To Not Resist.

In such a Circumstance The Divine „Feels" Most Tenderly „Invited", To Recognize Itself As You. And It Will „Do" Exactly That. In Its Self-Sensing Majestic Fullness, As Spanda, It Will Self-Sense Itself As You, As The „Dazzling" Sun Of Love. And then? Oh, then...

Radiant Spirit-Bliss „will" take over then. It „Will" Reveal and Run, what needs to be and happen and Self-Sense and Shine.

17. Radiant Existence

17.1

The Secret Of Order in the midst of turbulences and of the chaos of „reality" Is neither pleasant nor disturbing; It Is Liberating. But What Is It?

17.2

It is your all-consuming and timeless native desire and nature, to be your nature AND Nature, Which Is Free, Ecstasy-Saturated, „Wildest" AND Most Blissful Absoluteness.

17.3

„Wildest" AND Most Blissful Absoluteness Is The Most Real In-Love-State. But It „Hides" in self-created dreaminess...

17.4

A dream is an involuntary experience during sleep and sleep is an involuntary and unconscious or dreamy-conscious state.

17.5

To get liberated from *spiritual* sleepiness, the exercise of the Science Of Disillusionment is indispensable.

17.6

The Science of Disillusionment consists in Distinguishing Truth from Maya.

17.7

Whatever is perceived, whenever it's perceived, i.e. felt and experienced, anything, it is Maya, a transcendental dream, because it happens involuntarily and because it's a hypnotic distraction from The Most Real. To even begin to sense or intuit this, is Ecstasy; let alone Realize it, Which Is Total Bliss.

17.8

Enlightenment Is Not: what you believe it is, what you think it is, what you feel it is, what you intuit it is, what you desire it is.

17.9

Enlightenment Breathes you, „Destroys" you, Sustains you, „Constitutes" you, Pervades you, Saturates you, Ecstasizes you, Exists you and Is you In and As Love-Absoluteness.

17.10

Maya (Sanskrit for „the world as illusion") is not an illusion. It is real and true. But not Most Real. Not Most True. Only a manifestation of The Most Real and True.

17.11

„Your" „self" is a manifestation of The Most Real and True as well.

17.12

When you Most Priorly and Transcendentally See through Maya and „your" „self"-condensed „you" or

"I" and breathe both Inside Out, Most Priorly and Infinitely Beyond, You restart Existing as Most Blissful and Love-"Flooded" Saturated Transparency Ad Infinitum. You restart Breathing In The "Rhythm" Of Ecstasy.

17.13

This Ecstasy is Beyond words, thoughts, feelings, states and any other experiences whatsoever.

17.14

It Is a human organism's psychoplastic and "self"-forgotten breathing Transparency, Which Allows Transcendental Organismicity; through Self-Forgetfulness and Total Psychophysical and All-Inclusive Existential Onticity or Beingness.

17.15

There is nothing more heart-breaking, "core"-melting, confinement-dissolving, mind-"exploding" or all-liberating compared to This Inconceivable and Most Obvious Freedom as Bliss;

This Eternal "Explosion" Of The Unbearable Bliss-Fullness Of What Everything and All Is:

An Unmoved "Fountain"-Sphere Of Boundlessly Lucid And Shining Luminosity.

17.16

There's no way to *conceive* This Radiant ...Bliss, This Unbounded Openness; an Openness from Every possible point in space at once to Every possible direction at once.

17.17

Yet, if you get a glimpse of That, or rather, if you taste It a bit, you will not want anything else *more* ...ever again.

17.18

In Fact, wanting as such will be functionalized for the organism's energetic-cyclic necessities alone and will not be activated anymore as a means for Existentially Transcendental Satisfaction, since this is an impossibility.

17.19

The most „impossible", most unique Characteristic of The State Of Radiant Bliss-Fullness, of This Reality As The Heart Of Everything, is Its Self-Generated, Perpetually New and Transcending-The-Former Ecstasy.

17.20

Not normal ecstasy, as if you would stand out of something or out of yourself, but an *Enstatic* Ecstasy.

17.21

Maybe the most suitable name or linguistic expression or verbal description for This State, for This Amazement, ...for what we Are and for what everything Is Totally, ...the most suitable form in words for It would be ‚Radiant Saturation'.

17.22

Free, Unbounded, Blissful and Transparent Radiant Saturation. Impossible to feel...

17.23

What is possible though is only your perpetual „sacrifice" – what is possible is „sacrificing" your „self"; the permanent state of being consumed, yet ...reborn.

17.24

Not even as a process, but your being perpetually reborn without any state in between of getting reborn and having a break and ...getting reborn again – no. It's the State of being reborn or born all the time; perpetually...

17.25

It's Self-Existing, Self-Generating Bliss, Radiantly Saturating Everything And Being It at the same time, at the same instant.

17.26

In A „Flow" ...Of Instant; Of Eternal Space.

17.27

As A Flow of a Tacit and Causeless Celebratory Eternity.

Nityananda Of Ganeshpuri

The Chidakash Sutras

Few days before my first visit to Ganeshpuri and in the feeling of my spiritually deep and prior connection to Bhagavan Nityananda of Ganeshpuri, I spontaneously wrote a commentary on six key verses from the Chidakash Gita, which on the one hand reveal The Nature and Structure Of Spiritual Reality and on the other hand emphasize the necessary body-mind-transcending Understanding and Realization for Spiritual Liberation.

Bhagavan Nityananda, free from every possible intention of being a scholar or pandit, was mainly and firstly a very physical, corporeal and Shakti-Full bodily manifestation of Satchitananda, The Feast Of The Utmost Delight Of Identification Of Shakti With Parashakti, Of Oneness Of All Prior and Secondary Forms With Their Formless, but Fullest Nature. This Oneness Is What Truth Is.

Nevertheless the Chidakash Gita, many of Bhagavan Nityananda's spoken words collected in a coherent sequence of verses by one of his „disciples", contains innumerable Tattvas, Truth Principles of The Highest Spiritual Value.

18. The Chidakash Sutras

A Shankara Commentary On Six Verses from the Chidakash Gita by Bhagavan Nityananda Of Ganeshpuri.

„SAT is the one, indivisible. It is the one ‚subtle' which is everlasting. CHIT is always changing." (111)

The Ineffable Transcendental Domain, Which Is The Most Obvious and Unmanifest *Whole Of Everything As One*, Is ONE *Inherently* and *Actually*.

As The Most Obvious and Unmanifest Whole Of Everything As One, SAT Is Indivisible, *both* logically and *without a conceivable* reason.

„Inside" SAT everything manifest arises as the Expression of Its Fullness. An outside is *impossible*.

„Inside" SAT CHIT is SAT's Emergence As *Feeling* Capacity, Effusion Of Ecstatic Love through SAT's Own Touch *With Itself*.

Touched by Its manifest variations, As CHIT, SAT Is *Ever* Free. Every Touch Is „*Inside*" Itself.

SAT's manifest variations always arise and disappear, thus always changing the Content Of CHIT.

„When the ‚SAT' unites with ‚CHIT', the result is Ananda. This Ananda is the Satchitananda, Sri Nityananda, Sri Paramananda. Union of Jiva and Paramatma is Ananda, Yogananda, Paramananda, Satchitananda and Brahmananda." (112)

Bliss *Untold*, Paramananda, Is The Self-Love-Radiance, Which Shines Eternally, Nitya, and „Occasionally", both without a conceivable reason and also due to the *Union*, Yoga, Of SAT or The *Most Obvious* Transcendental Absolute, Brahman, With One, More Or All Of Its *Individuated* Feeling Manifestations.

Jiva Is An Individuated Feeling Manifestation Of *Infinite* Feeling Potential: Paramatma.

Union Of Jiva and Paramatma Is The Fullness-Inherent *Celebratory Impulse* Of The Divine, *Advaya*.

Satchitananda Is The Feast Of The *Utmost Delight* Of Identification Of Shakti With *Parashakti*, Of Oneness Of All Prior and Secondary Forms With Their *Formless*, but *Fullest Nature*. This Is *Truth*.

„One who has not realized the truth is a beggar. One who has not destroyed delusion, one who

has not left off the downward (worldly) path, is a beggar." (202)

Truth Is The *Coincidence* Of What Is Manifest With Its *Unmanifested* Nature. It Is The Untraceable *Union* Of SAT and CHIT As *One*.

Being (through delusional *false* identification) *deprived* of Mukti, of SAT's *Most* Sublime Freedom-Bliss and Acausal Radiant *Fullness*, a manifest feeling individuation or sentient being is cut off from The *Only Possible Complete* Satisfaction.

Ever hungry and existentially unsatisfied and *unhappy* the separated being gets caught up in the trap of *identifying with the body-mind* and thus in the sisyphean machinery of *will*.

No matter what one's will's fulfillments satisfy, as long as Truth as *Satchitananda* is *not* The Case, *wanting* (Transcendentally) is *begging*.

„One who has thoroughly wiped off the idea ‚I am the body' is fit to be called a Guru. There is none higher than such a one. There is no God above such a Guru. Such a Guru is God, and God is such a Guru." (29)

Understanding (Transcendentally) the *essence* of conditional identification *initiates* Liberation.

Being a body-mind is real, but not *Most* Real. It is a vibrational *addition* Out Of and Inside The Most Real.

Vibrating Freely Or Feeling Unconditionally As The Total Body-Mind *unleashes* the body-mind as individuated feeling manifestation from its conditional bondage and liberates it back into The *Translucent* Functionality it Truly *Is*.

Only *Such* Translucent Functionality Grants True and Direct Divine Agency.

Such Is The *SAT-Guru's Function* As The Divine *Agent*.

„If you perform tapas for thousands of years with the desire for results, it is of no avail. But if you perform tapas for one ghatika (twenty-four minutes) without any desire for ‚fruits', you will see ALL in God and God in ALL." (66)

Spiritual Practice can *never* be a means for conditional achievement or satisfaction.

The tapas delusion as a means for achieving is necessarily futile. Practice, which is *applied in order to achieve*, essentially doesn't change anything of truly spiritual value.

True Tapas Is The *Self-Evident* Purification of a body-mind from its conditional *stickiness*.

Such Self-Evident Purification *Activates* Itself, When Shining Grace „Kisses" and „Enters" a feeling (human) conditionality As Divine *Shaktipat*.

True Tapas Is The Fruit *Of Itself, Already* Divine, Perfectly *Full*.

True Tapas Is Divine Shaktipat *Unfolding*. Most Attractive, Self-Satisfying, Truth As Free Action.

„All Tattvas have one root Tattva called Parabrahma. When this is realized, it is called Jivan Mukti. You must see the river at its source and not after it merges into the sea. You should see the mother root of a tree. All the trees have one mother root. So also, all have one and only one God. When you have realized all as one homogeneous, this realization is Mukti." (219)

Rather than through the goal of *unification* with The Divine, a goal, which arises out of the separation *from* the Divine, Liberation, Jivan Mukti, „Requires" A Radical Transcendental *Recognition*.

It Is The *Divine*, Which Recognizes *Itself* inside an additional modification Of Its Very Formless Radiant Fullness.

Everything manifest is a Divine *Modification*, a modification of *The Same*, of The Very *One, Inside* of

Which *surrender* can *open*.

Such Divine Self-Recognition *Is* Mukti. Love Untold. Bliss Supreme.

Such Divine *Self*-Recognition Makes True and Natural Surrender *Possible* and *Inevitable*.

Epilogue: Truth And Grace

1.1.1

Truth Is (among other things) the Coincidence of a belief, a perception or an understanding with *Reality*.

1.1.2

The truth with Truth though is, that (in the dimension of appearances) It Is *not* the Principle that governs the human world.

1.2.1

Emotion is (among other things) the more or less pleasant or unpleasant quality or inner existential atmosphere of a living being's feeling.

1.2.2

The truth with (and in fact: reactive and unnatural) emotion is, that it is the *actual* principle that governs the human world.

1.3.1

The Moment Truth „*will*" *attract most* of all genuine emotion of human beings, at This Moment True Spiritual Transformation will have started.

1.3.2

Realized Spiritual Life Is The *Opposite* of the reign of reactive emotion over truth; It Is the naturally spontaneous expression of true emotion *In* Truth.

2.1

Truth Is (among other „things") The Quality Of Existence Itself, Of Being-There Pure, Of Being-There Free, Of Being-There Whole-As-One-And-All.

2.2

There may be needs for living beings, yet Truth-As-Existence-Unveiled Is The *Only True Need*, because *It Alone Satisfies* a living being's organismic and existential totality and reality.

2.3

Intuition or Taste of Truth-As-Existence-Unveiled or shy Reality Baptism triggers unmistakenly The Great Process <u>towards</u> and <u>No Return</u> from Self-Recognized Divinity.

2.4

Self-Recognized Divinity Is The Groundless Infinity-Heart-Bliss to Eat and Drink from and Rest In and Be As – in The Eternal Manner, Reality Intoxicated.

2.5

Between triggering and accomplishing Total and Full Reality Baptism, between opening shyly and allowing Radiant Light Infinity tracelessly, may lie seconds or aeons, meters or light years.

2.6

The stickier the identification with manifested reality-as-needs-and-modes-of-existence, the more indispensable Grace becomes; along with all prerequisites necessary for „Flirting" With Grace Successfully and „Helping" Her Embrace you and Explode you out of your experiential „chaos" and Into Her Ecstatic Majesty.

3.1

Spirituality in the Sense of *Spirit as Kundalini Mahashakti* is the *understanding* and expressively *being* of „oneself" and the world as Spontaneous Ecstatic Manifestation of Self-Consuming Self-Generated Paramrita Spanda Bliss-Fullness in the *Holistic, All-Encompassing, All-Inclusive* and *All-Embracing* Manner.

3.2

Spirituality in the Sense of *Spirit as Kundalini Mahashakti* Is *The* Reason for an Eternal Celebration or Most Ecstatic Traceless Transcendental Free Vibration, because It does not need any conditional or generated reasons for celebration or enjoyment, since everything conditional or generated – all forms and manifestations of suffering included – is a manifestation of The Unconditional First and Last and Only Condition Of <u>Radiant Paramrita Spanda</u> *Being And Expression.*

3.3

Spiritual Life and Existence in the Sense of *Spirit as Kundalini Mahashakti* Is The Complete or Ever Magnifying *Embodiment* and *Lived Reality* Of All That (or Ever More Of What) Truthfully Is *As* It Truthfully Is Through *Paramrita Spanda <u>Shaktipat</u>* Or <u>*Transmissional Infusion*</u> and Eventually <u>*Traceless Saturation*</u>.

3.4

Spanda *Is* Everything. And In *Different* Manners At *Once*. Reality, Both In Her Conditional Manifestations And In Her Free And Unbound Infinity Fullness, Is (Paramrita) Spanda.

3.5

„This" Spanda Has Many Faces. *Radiant Ecstasy Untold* Is Her *Bliss* Face. *Truth* Is Her *Quality* And *Clarity* Face. *Grace* Is Her *Embracing* Face.

3.6

Finding Her Quality and Clarity Is *Becoming* and Eventually *Being* Truth And *As* Truth, Which In Itself Is What „Opens" Her Grace.

„Opening" Her Grace Is Finding Her Embrace, Which (Ever More And Eventually) Is Transparently And Tracelessly Shining Love-Blissful Saturation and Completeness Or Undivided Absoluteness.

Such A State, Which *Is* The *True* State *Of* Everything And *As* Everything, *Is* Her State: Spanda*bhava*.

Such A Realm, Which *Is* The *True* Realm *Of* Everything And *As* Everything, *Is* Her Realm: Spanda*loka*. The Real World In Its True Freedom And In Its True Light.

In The Mouth Of Her Light

THE LIGHT
OF THE WORLD

The Light of the world
Is not definable;
not because
there are no words
to talk with about It,
but because
It Inherently Dissolves
the „infinity" of the mind's capacity
and its conditionally limited magnitude
In Divine Mindlessness,
Worldlessness
and Paramrita Spanda Bliss.

This Light has never been described.
This Light Is Ever Beyond.
This Light Is Ever Prior.

Please don't become deluded by Maya
in thinking that you understand.
You cannot understand This Light.
It cannot be understood.
It Only Fully Is.
It Only Is Fullness.
Infinity.
I-n-f-i-n-i-t-y.
Unimaginable Infinity.
Unbearably Ecstatic Otherworld.
Infinitely Blissful.

What you can do?
Surrender.
Fully.
Forget the world.
„Lose" yourself.
And Then Awaken As The Here,
The Everywhere,
The Inside Out
and All The Marvels
Of Transcendental Boundlessness
and Love.

The Spanda Grand

Deep „Inside",
Really „Deep",
in a „Merciless"
and Infinitely Wildful-Free
Sense Of Deep,

When „Inside"
Is Ontically Conceived
Outside the realm
of the body-mind traps
or conditional prejudice
As The Inside-Out-
-Of-Everywhere-And-All-
-Ground-Existential-Substance-
-Of-No-Priorly-Before,

When „Inside" Is „Outside",
When Space Of Who
Is Not A Where, But Is
An As
Eternal-Undivided Heart,

As „Dark" As Perfect Light,
As „Bright" As Perfect Love,
As Free As Throat Gone Lost,
As Chest „Outblown" In All,
As Belly Unconfined,
In Such A Sense Of Deep „Inside",

A „Fire" „Burns",
A „Water" „Sweet",
A „Weeping" Holy,
A Joy „Raw",
A Being Forever,
A Bliss-Full Stand.
The Spanda Grand.

Spanda

Invocation

„I" open up
and raise „my" breath
and let it fall
in and dissolve
In Priorness and Utmost Free and Utmost Full
and Unborn Blissful One.

The body breath and bonded mind
an open wound and tuning in
to Totally Beyond.

The Kiss Of Grace
Melts every trace
of borderlines In Being,
The Glorious No-Thing.

Pure Absoluteness Flowering
Ever Above
and Always In
Beloved's Tender Rain,
Intimate Wedding's Love and Pain,
...Unbearable Embrace.

Sweet Spanda Light,
Most Precious „Sight",
Lost, Vanished Me
Most Tenderly
In Your Abysmal
Shine Of Face.

The Stages Of The Realization Process

The Transcendental Spiritual Realization (and Liberation) Process, as It Is Implied and Meant in this book, should not be confused with some kind of therapy or education for achieving or fulfilling something that can only be achieved and fulfilled by a right and balanced life according to the laws of reality and the healthy possibilities of the respective culture.

Of course It can also have and has many therapeutical-healing or educational-instructive beneficial effects for a right and balanced life, yet this is not Its Primary Field Of Operating Manifestation and Transfiguration.

It works best and is more suitable for all who cannot help but step forward; towards The Truth Of Their Nature. In this case, it is of great advantage to be grounded in the conscious responsibility necessary for a right and balanced life, whether totally or at least partially, but surely on the way.

What is the nature and the anatomy of the Transcendental Spiritual Realization (and Liberation) Process? In Its Essence It Is The Conscious Process that allows existing, living and being as an expression of The Transcendental and Radiant Reality Itself.

Spirituality can be defined in different ways. Therefore the terms or notions ‚spirituality' and ‚spiritual' do not always refer to the same.

The term ‚spiritual' is used by me in the Sense of *Spirit as Kundalini Mahashakti*, Which Is The Vibrant

Force, Field Or Space As Main and First Agent Of <u>Radiant Paramrita Spanda</u>, Which Is The First And Transcendentally Free And Everything Else Generating and Containing Reality. The Conscious Process that allows existing, living and being as an expression of The Transcendental and Radiant Reality Itself, consists of and in the following stages.

1. Intuition and Longing

The first Stage creates the space, in which the nature of the impulse for most True Realization can be detected, intuited and discovered in Its Most Attractive Force.

This first stage is decisive, because illusions of confusing the Spiritual Process for yet another consolation strategy for problems or unfulfilled needs of a conditionally imbalanced life can undermine the activation and the course of the Liberating Process.

2. Initiation and Understanding

The second Stage aims at the discovery and understanding of the fabric of Reality in both its logic, its conditional ordeal and its ecstasy; at the discovery of all that can and has to be understood. This is complex and simple at once. Complex, because the facets of being human are innumerable. And simple, because it is fueled by Love, Life Force and Radiant Reality Itself.

What needs to be understood in this stage, is Reality Itself (a) In Its Unlimited Entirety and (2) In Its „Operational" and „Behavioral" Ways.

3. Practicing and Living

In the third Stage now the practice of all that has been discovered and understood in the second stage takes place as practicing or spiritually awakened conscious living until its fulfilled ripeness. So that Realization „waits" „outside" and maybe already „knocks at the door"...

This Stage is the Heart of The Spiritual Process, since it is here, where the Real Transfiguration takes place.

4. Realization and Shine

This Stage is not a Stage. It is a coming together. Language and rationality fail to describe it. Nevertheless it can be said, it is the place and space, in which all who demonstrate all of stage three with less and less irritation come together and just are together in this demonstration. Realization is possible at any moment; even if its expectation may not even arise anymore...

5. Spandaloka and Beyond

In this „stage" there is the discovery and enjoyment of what is and how it is, when more come and are together after Realization. It is about The Culture Of Radiant Reality Itself, Expressed As Its Realized Ecstatic Radiance, Truth, Fullness, and Free Vibrational Shine. It Is The Rise Of The Most Intimate, Of The Most Obvious, Of The Most Real; Of Spandaloka In Its Infinity.

Further Information

This Book Is A Description Of The
Transcendental Spiritual Realization
And Liberation Process And An Invitation
For Everyone Who Is Inevitably And
Truly Interested In Its Transformational
Force And Nature.

For further information about Shankara's
publications and His Spiritual Work
As A Whole, please visit our website.

---

www.shankaraloka.org

Copyright © 2016 Spandaloka Ltd.

All rights reserved. No part of this publication may be reproduced or transmitted in any form or by any means, electronic or mechanical, including photocopying, recording, or by any information storage and retrieval system, without permission in writing from Spandaloka Ltd.

Publisher: Spandaloka Ltd, Birmingham, Berlin.

Printed in Germany.

ISBN: 978-3-946224-01-3

www.shankaraloka.org

Bibliographic information published by the Deutsche Nationalbibliothek (German National Library): The Deutsche Nationalbibliothek lists this publication in the Deutsche Nationalbibliografie (German National Bibliography).

www.ingramcontent.com/pod-product-compliance
Lightning Source LLC
Chambersburg PA
CBHW060342170426
43202CB00014B/2854